USSR HUMOR

COMPILED BY CHARLES WINICK

WITH ILLUSTRATIONS BY

GRISHA DOTZENKO

FOR THE PETER PAUPER PRESS

MOUNT VERNON, N. Y.

INTRODUCTION

THIS collection of the best folk humor of the Soviet Union reflects some themes that are universal, others that reflect a planned society with some dissatisfactions, and some themes that stem from Russia's being a Communist country. Another group of themes can only be described in terms of the unique national character of the Russian people. In spite of its origins and the special context in which it appears, Russian humor is very similar to much American humor.

The Russian word anekdot means a funny story; most of the contents of this book are anekdoty. There are some examples of the shutka, or jest. By far the greatest proportion of the funny stories are passed on by word of mouth, from community to community and even across national boundaries. By its very nature, much of this folk humor enjoys an underground existence, because it is anti-regime. It emerges in reports from travelers, students, guides, and others.

Krokodil, the bi-weekly official Soviet magazine of satire, usually directs its ironic barbs at bureaucrats and at the behavior of the average Russian. Krokodil receives an average of 800 letters a day from its readers, complaining of corruption and shortcomings. Its contents are very contemporary but do not satirize leaders like Premier Khrushchev, in spite of his well known interest in poking fun.

Krokodil derives its name from a story by Dostoevski. Many other Russian writers have used humor effectively and even brilliantly. Funny stories that deal with politics date back at least as far as Peter the Great. Even many of the best known early Russian fairy tales are in the form of funny stories. Russians take pride in telling anekdoty. And their pride is justified, because such stories and jokes in the USSR represent a uniquely sensitive and truly folk form of humor. They provide a continuingly available source of informal comment on events, institutions, and personalities of the Soviet Union. They also furnish an escape valve for the expression of feelings that may have difficulty in finding other outlets.

CHARLES WINICK

When Stalin died, he went to Heaven and knocked at St. Peter's door. St. Peter asked, "What do you want here?" Stalin replied, "I want to come in." St. Peter answered, "No, you go to Hell." The following day, fifteen devils knocked on the door to Heaven and St. Peter asked them what they wanted. The devils said, "We are the first refugees."

Premier Khrushchev got tired of all of the barbs directed at him because of the plight of the Jews in the Soviet Union. He decided to attempt to generate a more favorable attitude toward the Soviet Union in terms of its treatment of Jews. He called in the Chief Rabbi of Moscow and asked him to send a letter to the Chief Rabbi of Israel, and to make this letter a positive statement about the situation of the Jews in the Soviet Union, and of how well they were treated. The Rabbi prepared such a letter and a carbon copy went to Khrushchev. When Khrushchev saw it, he was puzzled and irritated at the postcript which read, "P.S. We have no candles and no sugar." Khrushchev called in the Rabbi and asked him why he had included the postscript, although the rest of the letter was very favorable. The Rabbi told Khrushchev: "Naturally, they will be suspicious if the letter sounds too perfect. Therefore, I made the letter very positive but I deliberately put in a few things that are negative in order to make the basic letter more believable." Khrushchev was satisfied with this explanation. When the Rabbi in Israel received the letter, he went to Premier Ben Gurion to discuss it. Ben Gurion asked the Rabbi, "What is the meaning of this letter? Why does he put in this little postscript about the unavailability of these two items? Who cares whether they're available, if the other things are so attractive for them?" The chief Rabbi said, "But my dear Premier, don't you see what he is saying? He is saying that their life is bitter and dark."

There was a campaign in Moscow for the police to be more courteous and friendly, in order to eliminate unpleasant recollections of the secret police. One day, a man sneezed in the subway. A policeman who was in the car asked, "Who sneezed?" The passengers were frightened by the policeman and nudged the person who had sneezed and urged him to confess. He did. The policeman pushed the other passengers aside, and said to the man who had sneezed, "Here's to your good health."

When God created Adam he gave him guidance on living and said, "You are Adam, the first man on earth. Go forth and do that which I have ordered." Adam went forth. The Creator was then astounded, on taking a look at Paradise, to see another man was already there. "Man," He called, "who are you?" "Me?" came the reply, "I am a Russian."

At a meeting of delegates from Communist countries in Moscow, each of the delegates noticed that there was a tack on his seat. The Czech delegate sat on his tack and smiled. The Polish delegate removed the tack from his seat and sat down with a pained expression. The Chinese removed the tack from his seat and placed his own tack on the seat. It read, "Made in China."

Two officials of Omsk were inspecting an orphanage. One asked the head of the orphanage, "What is the daily allowance for the children at this orphanage?" The official answered. "The allowance, sir, is two rubles a month." The official ordered, "Well, let's cut that in half to one ruble a month." The two officials then went on to visit a jail and asked what the allowance for prisoners was in the jail. The warden replied, "One ruble every three months." The first official snapped, "Let's change that to two rubles a month." The two officials left the jail, and one said, "I am surprised that you would take away from children and give to criminals." The other answered, "Well, I'm just looking out for our interests and anticipating where we will be spending our old age. We're not likely to be spending it in a nursery."

What is the difference between comedy, tragedy, and socialist realism? Comedy was before the war when you had a girl and couldn't afford to take her out. Tragedy was during the war when you couldn't find a girl and there was no place to take her. Socialist realism is now when you have a girl and you can take her out but you never have time because you always have to go to a Party meeting.

Some years ago, an American and a Russian were discussing the relative merits of their respective leaders. The American felt that Hoover was a greater man than Stalin because "he taught the Americans not to drink." The Russian thought for a moment and said, "Well, that is true, but Stalin, after all, taught the Russians not to eat."

When Stalin was in office, he once noted that there were mice in his study and complained to President Kalinin about this. The President thought for a moment and suggested, "Why don't you put up a sign reading 'Collective Farm'? Half the mice will die of hunger and the other half will run away."

A citizen of the Soviet Union and of West Germany arrived in Hell. They were surprised to discover that there were separate places for them. They decided to investigate the areas to which they were assigned and then to come back and discuss their relative merits in a month. The man from the West wanted to persuade his friend in the Eastern Hell to escape and to defect. He described life in Western Hell as something glamourous. "We have a bad life only during the day when we are fried in sulphur and tar. Our evenings and nights are wonderful. We are free and have a great time in the bars and dance halls." The Russian citizen, however, was unimpressed. He said that he preferred the Hell managed by the Soviet Union. "We are never fried here. When we have to creep into the furnaces, there is usually a shortage of tar. If there is tar, then there is usually a shortage of sulphur. If there is a stock of both, then there is no coal. Only once did it happen that we had a stock of all three ingredients. This was such a remarkable event that the comrade devils immediately convened a conference and had to attend it. You see, our Hell is much better than yours."

A Russian diplomat was negotiating a loan for his country from an American diplomat. The American asked, "What is your security for the loan?" The Russian answered, "Our vast deposits of gold, iron, and coal." "But," the American objected, "Those are all below the ground. What security do you have above it?" "The government of the Soviet Union and its leaders," was the reply. "Very well," the American answered. "We will give you a loan when what is below the ground is above it and when what is now above it goes below."

An interviewer once asked Karl Radek whether he believed in the multi-party system. Radek answered, "Of course, I am a genuine democrat and do believe in a multi-party system. I believe that there must be several parties. I believe in having one party in power and in having the other parties in jail."

At a concentration camp in Siberia some years ago, several inmates were talking with each other about why they were in the camp. One said, "I am here for saying that Karl Radek was a counter-revolutionary." The second said, "Isn't that interesting. I am here for saying that he was not a counter-revolutionary." They turned to the third man and asked, "What are you here for?" He answered, "I am Karl Radek."

A resident of Soviet Lithuania was talking to a friend from another part of Russia about his community. He said, "It's wonderful and I'm so proud to be in a city of the new Lithuania, which is the largest country in the world." His friend asked, "How do you figure that?" He answered, "Well, our Western frontier is on the Baltic Sea, our capital is in Moscow, and the majority of our population is in Siberia."

A Party member went fishing with a non-Party friend. Presently, the non-Party member began to haul in fish after fish while the Party man caught none. "Why are you catching so many when I haven't even had a nibble?" asked the Communist. "Simple," said his friend. "Seeing that Party badge in your lapel, even the fish are afraid to open their mouths."

There was a sign in the window of a Kiev bakery: "Man does not live by bread alone."

There was a competition for a statue to the great Russian poet Alexander Pushkin, during the regime of Joseph Stalin. At the unveiling of the prize statue, many persons were surprised to see that the statue that won the prize consisted of a huge representation of Stalin reading a small volume of Pushkin's poems.

Premier Stalin decided to go incognito to a movie, to get some impressions of the temper of the people. He was enjoying the film and then a newsreel appeared and he saw his own picture on the screen. There was tremendous applause in the theater and almost everybody in it stood up. Stalin, however, modestly maintained his seat. The man next to him nudged him and said, "You know, most people feel the way you do. But it would be safer to stand."

Two Russian Santa Clauses were talking to one another. "Tell me," said one, "do you believe in children?"

An official said, "Here, comrade, is your free pass to the asylum." "No, thank you, I want to take my vacation in another place, not in an asylum. I am perfectly normal." "No normal person would refuse a free pass."

14

Stalin and his party were visiting an insane asylum and there was tremendous applause after the speech by Stalin to the group. The police who accompanied the dictator noted that there were several people off to the side who were not applauding. They went over to them and asked them why they were not. "Oh, we are not the patients — we work here," was their reply.

A citizen had presented himself at a government office and was irritated at the treatment he was getting. He said, "I want attention." The clerk answered, "For attention, apply at Room 8, which is open every other day from 4 to 5 in the afternoon."

A Siberian peasant went to Moscow in order to find out from Stalin himself the meaning of the phrase, "Stakhanovite Activist." Stalin told him. "You see that bus in the street? If ten buses run in an hour instead of one, we have the Stakhanovite Activists to thank for it." The peasant went home, called his friends together, and pointed to a hearse that happened to be passing. "See that?" he asked. "Well, if ten hearses pass in an hour instead of one, we have the Stakhanovite Activists to thank for it."

15

A Russian worker was asked at a Party meeting how many shirts he had before the Communists came into power. "Two," was his answer. "And probably made of the cheapest material," the Party man prompted. The worker nodded. "And how many shirts do you have now?" asked the official smugly. "One," replied the worker. "Ah," said the Party man after a pause, "but probably made of far better material than the sort they offered the workers in the bad old days. Tell us what is your shirt made of?" The worker shifted his feet. "Well," he said at length, "it's made out of what I could salvage of the original two."

Mikoyan had wanted to ship Stalin's body to Israel. "We had better not do so," said Khrushchev. "I seem to recall that Israel is the place where someone rose from the dead a long time ago."

On leaving a building, the head of the Secret Police Beria fell down the stairs. His secretary rushed to a telephone and called Beria's doctor. "Hurry, Doctor," she said, "I think he has broken his backbone." "Nonsense," replied the doctor. "I have been treating him for many years and I know that he doesn't have one."

An advisor came in to Premier Khrushchev very exultantly one day. "I can prove that Adam and Eve were Russian," he said. "We can now claim the invention of man along with our invention of radio, automobiles, telephone and television." Khrushchev asked, "How? You know the United States likes to ridicule our claims in such matters and we must be very careful that we can document it." "I am completely confident," said the official. "Adam and Eve had no clothes, they had no roof over their heads and had only apples. Yet they thought they lived in Paradise. What else could they have been but Russians?"

Stalin had convened a meeting of the Politburo, and found that his briefcase containing his secret papers had disappeared after the meeting. He could not find the papers anywhere. Stalin was enraged and telephoned Beria, the head of the secret police. He said, "My briefcase with secret papers must have been stolen during the meeting of the Politburo. I want you to arrest every single member of the Politburo until you find it." The next morning, while going through his papers, Stalin found his briefcase. He called Beria and told him to release all the members. Beria said, "I'm terribly sorry, it's too late. Every single one has confessed."

Two Russian workers were talking about how near they were to socialism. One said, "The Party told me that socialism is on the horizon. I didn't know just what that meant. So I looked it up in the dictionary and read that a horizon is an imaginary line which moves further away from you as you approach it."

Two Russians were chatting about a mutual friend: "Whatever became of Ivan?" "Oh, he's changed jobs. He used to steal in the shoe store, but now he steals in the tailor shop."

A lawyer, a doctor and a psychoanalyst arrived in Heaven. The lawyer and doctor had a difficult time in clarifying their reasons for admittance, but after a considerable discussion they finally proved that they did many good deeds on earth and were admitted. But St. Peter immediately clutched the psychoanalyst's arm and hurried him right in, as soon as the lawyer and doctor had gone. "You're just the man we've been looking for," he confided, "we need your services. The Almighty is suffering from a delusion. He thinks he's Stalin."

The house of an old peasant straddled the Russian-Polish border. The local Soviet official had tried for some time to woo the peasant in order to get him to declare his house to be completely Russian so that the rent revenues from the building would be completely Russian. He had sent the peasant gifts and in many other ways sought to ingratiate himself with him. Finally, he felt that the time had come to reap the benefits of his energetic application.

He called on the peasant and told him, "Well, my dear comrade, I am sure that you have frequently had occasion to consider the silliness of having your home in two different countries. I think that the time has come for you to stop this ambiguous situation and to opt for either Russia or Poland, as your homeland. I am pretty sure that I know which you will decide, but I would like to hear it from your own lips. Well now, tell me, which country do you want to have your house in?" The Russian peasant did not hesitate a moment: "Well, there is no doubt in my mind that I want my house to be in Poland." The Soviet official was thunderstruck, and asked: "But why? Why?" The peasant answered, "It's very simple. I just simply can't stand another one of those Russian winters."

After his death, Stalin was greeted at the gates of Heaven and taken on a tour by St. Peter. Stalin found the quiet and pious life of the people there disagreeable, and requested permission to go to Hell. Complying with his wish, St. Peter took him to the gates of Hell and handed him over to Lucifer. Stalin was led to a noisy bar, where there was much revelry and dancing going on. "This is for me," declared Stalin, but Lucifer's reply was to lead him into the kitchen where he was popped into a kettle of boiling oil. Stalin protested and asked to be returned to the bar. "Brother," replied Lucifer, "that was just propaganda!"

A Soviet citizen had a talking parrot. One day, at the open window, the bird cried loudly, "Down with Khrushchev, down with the Communist Party." Someone reported the incident and the parrot's owner was ordered to Court. On the way to the Court, with his parrot under his arm, the man met a priest and told him of his problem. "Never mind," said the priest. "I too have a speaking parrot and we can exchange birds for the trial." So the man appeared in Court with the priest's parrot. The judge said to the parrot, "Now let us hear: 'Down with Khrushchev, down with the Communist Party.'" Answered the priest's parrot: "May God hear our prayers."

Beria and Stalin arrived at the gates of Heaven. St. Peter looked them over and said, "Whoever has done bad things on earth should step forward and prepare for the trip to Purgatory." Beria stepped forward. "Come along," St. Peter said. "And don't leave that deaf man behind."

A student asked in class, "Why is the Kremlin wall so high?" His teacher answered: "To keep the scoundrels from crossing it." "From the Kremlin?" asked the student.

When Stalin's corpse was removed from its tomb in Red Square, Lenin woke up and asked, "What's going on here?" Stalin replied happily, "I'm fed up with sharing a room. The housing situation has eased up and I'm going to get a place of my own."

The teacher asked little Fyodor: "Who is your father?" "The great Stalin," he replied. "And who is your mother?" He replied obediently: "The Soviet Union." The teacher continued: "And what would you like to be when you grow up?" "An orphan," came the prompt reply.

Radio Armenia reported that Lenin one day brought flowers for his colleague Stalin in the tomb. Stalin accepted the flowers, as a tribute to his greatness. "Not at all," Lenin answered. "What do you think, that I am giving you the flowers because of your greatness? I'm giving them to you because you're really dead."

When Malenkov was appointed, an elderly peasant woman innocently wrote to him to congratulate him on the new position. "I wish you everything," she wrote, "that the Russian people wished for Stalin during his lifetime." The next day, she was arrested for instigation to murder.

Two men met in prison and were surprised to see each other. One asked the other, "What are you in here for? The last I heard you had tremendous prestige within the Communist Party in Moscow." "Yes, you are right, I was a high Party official, but I made a reform proposal. I worked out a plan for the Party to get a great many members within a very short time. I suggested that anyone who brings in one new Party member should not have to pay membership dues anymore, and that someone who got two Party members could quit the Party."

The Russian teacher was explaining the meaning of the comparatives in grammar. He said, "I think that I can explain it best if we take a simple adjective like the word 'good.' The first order is the word 'good.' The second order of comparison is the word 'better.' The third order of comparison is the word 'best.' The fourth is 'Soviet.'"

A class in Irkutsk was being conducted on the differences between Capitalism and Communism. The teacher asked the class, "What is the difference between these two forms of economy?" Little Misha answered, "Capitalism is the ruthless exploitation of man by man." The teacher said, "That is very good. Now, what is Communism?" Little Misha answered, "Vice-versa."

A Moscow class was studying the United States. The teacher asked one of the students: "Ivan, what is the United States like?" Ivan answered: "The United States is a Capitalist country which has millions of people unemployed and starving." The teacher said: "And what is the goal of the Soviet Union?" Ivan answered: "The goal of the Soviet Union is to catch up with the United States."

Each day a Russian worker left his factory pushing a wheelbarrow full of straw. Each day the guard halted him and carefully checked the straw but found nothing. After a month of this, the guard said to the worker, "Look, I am being sent to the Urals, so you can talk freely with me. I give you my word I won't tell. But I am curious — what have you been stealing?" "Wheelbarrows," confessed the worker.

"Who was the first man?" the teacher asked. "Our beloved Khrushchev, Comrade Teacher," said the student. "No, I didn't mean it like that," the teacher interjected. "The first man was Adam." "Well — yes," the surprised student answered, "if you want to count the Capitalists."

A school teacher in a large Soviet city asked her pupils "Why is there an increase in population here in this city?" A pupil answered: "There is an increase in the population because the people from the country come to the big city." The teacher said: "That is very good. Now, children, think carefully. What can be done to prevent the country population from coming to the city?" The same pupil answered: "Well, we could set up collective farms here, too."

The famous Academician Lysenko was conducting an experiment on the auditory nerves of the flea. He put a flea on his right hand and told it to jump to his left hand. It did. He then ordered it to jump back. It did. He then removed its hind legs, and commanded it to jump to the right. It did not. Lysenko smiled and said, "This proves scientifically that the flea loses its sense of hearing when its legs are removed."

26

At a workers' meeting, Comrade Ivan got up to ask a question: "How is it that we have such shabby clothes, even though we hear about the wonderful textiles that the Soviet Union is making?" The Chairman of the meeting said that he didn't know, but he would ask his superiors and have the answer ready at the next meeting. At the next meeting, the Chairman asked, "Is there anybody who would like to ask a question?" One man said, "I have a question to ask. Where is Ivan?"

What is the most boring Whodunit in the world? The most boring Whodunit is "The History of the Communist Party," because by the third page you know who committed the murders.

A Soviet teacher posed this question to his class. "How would you define Communism?" Little Nikita raised his hand. "Communism is a boat rocked on all sides, but it finally reaches its port." "Very good," said the teacher. Then he noticed Dmitri squirming in his seat. "You wish to add something, Dmitri?" Dmitri hesitated, and then blurted out, "Nikita forgot one thing. While the boat is being rocked, everybody on board is seasick."

A production expert in Moscow, in his efforts
to comply with the government's drive to save
equipment, submitted to the Ministry of Economic Affairs a plan for the cessation of manufacture of beds. "Beds have become obsolete,
since all Communists must remain vigilantly
awake day and night and reactionaries never
venture to fall asleep. The rest of the population

28

has come to the point where they keep their eyes constantly open anyway."

Two residents of Leningrad were discussing the fuel shortage in their city. One said, "Your house is always warm. How do you manage that?" The second man answered, "In strict confidence, it's my parrot. I bought a parrot and taught it to say 'Long live the Communist Party.' Then I put it out on a back balcony overlooking the wood depot. Whenever it shouts that slogan, the depot workers throw firewood at it. So now I get all the fuel I need."

A visitor from the West was listening to a factory manager talk about his production record. The manager said, "In our first year, we made five hundred units. In our second year, we made five thousand units. In our third year, we made 120,000 units. Next year, we expect to make 923,000 units." The visitor asked, "What do you manufacture?" The manager gave him a small tag on which the visitor read the legend, "The elevator isn't working — sorry."

A man walking down a Moscow street, spat on the curb. A voice behind him warned, "Please don't talk politics, Comrade."

There is a popular joke about the bottled medicine that is made by the state controlled pharmaceutical manufacturing firm. "If you follow the directions on the bottle," the saying goes, "you stand a good chance of recovering from your illness. These directions read 'Keep bottle tightly closed.'"

At a meeting of a collective farm group, prizes were being awarded for outstanding accomplishment. The milkmaid Anastasia received a prize of a hen and a rooster for caring for her hens so effectively. After the award was announced, there was much applause and music. It was then announced that Petrov the stable boy would get a new suit for having raised a very fine prize horse. There was tremendous applause and music in honor of his award. Finally, it was announced that shock brigade harvester Boris, for harvesting 390 percent more than his quota of grain, for working seven days a week, for his high political acumen, and for setting seventeen records for other workers to emulate, would get the grand prize — a complete set of the works of Lenin. There was no applause and no music, but from one corner of the large room could be heard the whisper of one peasant to another, "It serves him right."

A Ukrainian community had constructed a bridge. "If there is a bridge, there must be a watchman," the members of the town said. "But a watchman must have a salary." So they decided to get a treasurer and an accountant. The watchman, the treasurer, and the accountant had to be directed by somebody. So they appointed an administrator. Now there was an administration. An order came to reduce the personnel. So they discharged the watchman.

A judge in a Soviet Court was pronouncing sentence on a man who had called a high official an idiot. "Fifteen years is the sentence for calling the Minister an idiot," said the judge. The defendant's lawyer said, "But that crime is only punishable by six months." The judge replied, "The sentence is not for that offense, but for divulging a State Secret."

There had been an influx of peasants and persons from farm areas into a large city. The city was the capital of the province. The provincial government announced: "Measures have been taken to free the capital of all superfluous natives, in order to minimize the housing shortage. The government is not worried about the overcrowding of prisons as a result of this measure."

Mao Tse Tung sent a telegram to Khrushchev: "China starves. Please send food." Khrushchev replied to Mao: "Tighten your belts." Mao replied to Khrushchev: "Please send belts."

A Russian worker was walking along the street with a friend and remarked, "It's a rotten government." A guard seized him by the arm. "You are under arrest," said the guard. "What for?" answered the worker. "Because you said it is a rotten government." The citizen protested. "But I never said what government." "No good," returned the guard. "There is only one rotten government and you know it."

A teenage girl and a teenage boy were sitting in a park in Moscow and listening to the song of a nightingale. She said to him, "Do you like the song of that nightingale?" He replied, "Until I know who wrote the melody, I can say nothing."

At the news that the Russians had broken into space, there was panic. Saturn hid his ring and Venus disguised herself as an old witch.

A visitor called at the home of Gherman Titov, the Russian Cosmonaut, but found only a small boy at home. "Where is your father?" the visitor inquired. The little boy answered, "Oh, he's out in space — he'll be back in three hours." The visitor inquired further, "And where is your mother?" The little boy answered, "She's out shopping — she'll be back in six hours."

A Russian official was giving a talk in one of the Eastern European countries: "One of our Russian Cosmonauts will soon be on the moon." A member of the audience nudged the person sitting next to him and said: "What's the big deal about just one Russian leaving the country?"

A Soviet worker, lunching at his factory canteen, pushed away his plate in disgust. "This food isn't fit for pigs," he shouted. His fellow workers watched in nervous silence as the Party Supervisor walked over to him. "Comrade," said the Supervisor, "do you realize that you are talking about the food products of our glorious Peoples' Republic? This is the food that will help us to kill off the enemies of the Soviet Union!" The worker grunted sceptically: "How are you going to get them to eat it?"

A factory worker was being quizzed by the personnel committee of the factory to see if he were suitable for promotion to foreman. He answered all the technical questions accurately, and then was asked his father's occupation. "I'd rather not answer that," he said. "We must know the answer," said the official. Reluctantly, the worker explained that his father was a street sweeper. "Ah, that is a fine proletarian occupation," beamed the interrogator. He went on with other questions, and then asked the applicant what his mother's occupation was. He balked, but finally admitted that his mother was a washer-woman. "That's a really good proletarian background," commented the questioner and continued down the list. When the form was all filled in, the interviewer said, "You are certainly qualified for the job, but first we must know one thing. Why didn't you want to tell us about your father and mother?" "You see," said the worker, "I had my heart set on this job and was determined to get it on my own merit."

An office worker arrived late for work. He said: "Because I was late today, I am practicing self-criticism. But if I criticize myself twice, will you let me be late tomorrow?"

Two workers were discussing the difference between doing overtime work in Russia and in a Capitalist country. "It's very easy," said one worker. "In Russia, if you work overtime you get your name in the paper, your picture in the Communist Party publications, and you are praised by leaders of our glorious government. In the Capitalist countries, you don't get your name in the paper, you don't get your picture in the papers, and you are not praised by anybody. All you get is a lot of money."

At 2:00 A.M. in the middle of the night in Minsk, there was a knock on the door. "Don't be upset," said a voice. "It's only the janitor. It's only a fire in the building."

A visitor from abroad was arriving at the Moscow airport for the first time. While the customs personnel were looking through his luggage, the visitor spent his time looking at the various posters and propaganda displays in the office. A local policeman tried to explain them to him. "Over there is the hammer and sickle, the symbol of our efforts at construction. Then you see the rifle as the symbol of our military concentrations. And the peace dove symbolizes the camp of the honest peace fighters." The visitor answered, "Aha, I understand. To sum it up, it means construction of military concentration camps for honest peace fighters. Right?"

A Russian who had left the country during the Bolshevik Revolution of 1917 recently returned in order to see whether the Khrushchev reform policies were really as radical as they were said to be. He had told his friends that in writing home, he would use red ink for the truth and black ink for comments that were only designed for the censors. Soon after he arrived in Russia, his best friend got a long letter in which he presented a glowing picture of industrial progress, efficiency and freedom. The final sentence in his letter was "You can find here the best of everything — except red ink."

The woman said to the proprietor of the food store, "One herring please." "Fine," he said. "Would you like it with a guitar or a balalaika?"

Petrov, a bureaucrat in Moscow, complained to his superior at the office, "I hear on the radio that we're producing a lot of meat, milk and butter. Yet my refrigerator is always empty. What shall I do?" His superior answered: "Plug your refrigerator directly into your radio."

Ivan said, "If we are attacked by the West, our agents will carry atom bombs concealed in suitcases to Paris, New York, London, and all the other big cities of the Capitalist Imperialist world and destroy them. Lyof answered, "I guess we will have enough bombs, but how about suitcases?"

A worker in a small Russian town decided that the struggle to meet his quota and sustain himself was just too much. He decided to be arrested, so that in jail he would be taken care of in terms of food and lodging. He stole two rolls, and the police were called. They refused to arrest him, saying, "We know what it is to be hungry." He then stole some jewels from a jewelry shop. He made no attempt to conceal his theft, and was apprehended by the owners. Instead of reporting him to the police, they invited him to join their gang, so that he could make even more money. In despair, he went to a Communist Party rally and shouted, "Communists are killers and Khrushchev is a pig." No one paid any attention to what he said. After the meeting, its chairman came over to him and said, "You must be crazy. What if there were real Communists at this meeting?"

A citizen of Leningrad went to a clinic to see an eye and ear specialist. "We have an eye specialist and we have an ear specialist," he was told, "but no eye and ear specialist." "But that will not do," he replied, "mine is a combined malady. Every day my ears hear of the wonderful life we lead here in the USSR, but all my eyes see is poverty and secret police."

Two Communist officials were gambling when they were observed by a third. "Comrades," he said, "why don't you play a more intelligent game? Why don't you play chess?" "We don't know how to play chess," answered the gambling comrades. "Well, if you insist on gambling, then at least play for beans, not for money." "For beans, Comrade?" asked the gamblers suddenly turning pale. "The stakes would be too high!"

A communique from St. Peter reports that Picasso reached the heavenly gates and asked for admission. "How do I know you're Picasso?" St. Peter says. "Anyone can make the claim. Prove it." Picasso pulls up a fold of the Saint's robe, doodles a masterpiece, and is admitted. Maria Callas arrives and is challenged in the same way. She vocalizes a few glorious bars, and is gallantly welcomed. Then comes Nikita Khrushchev. When he objects to the challenge, St. Peter explains patiently that it is quite routine. "Picasso and Callas have just come in, and they were willing to prove their identity. Why shouldn't you?" "Picasso and Callas?" asks Khrushchev with interest. "Who are they?" "Come in, come in," says St. Peter. "You have proved you're Khrushchev."

A policeman brought a man before a Soviet Magistrate. He saluted the Magistrate and said, "This fellow has dangerous thoughts, your Honor." "What did he say?" "We grabbed him before he could say anything."

An old woman had formed the daily habit of running to the newsstand early in the morning to get the first copy of *Pravda*. She would buy it, take a glimpse at the front page headlines, crumple it up in disgust and tramp on it. She did this every day. Finally the news vendor could no longer restrain his curiosity. "If you don't want to read the paper, why do you rush down to buy it every morning? Newspapers are expensive." "I'm looking for a death notice," explained the old woman. "No wonder you'll never find it, old woman," said the vendor. "Don't you know death notices are always printed on the back page?" "Not the death notice I'm looking for," said the woman.

In Moscow, the streetcar conductor called, "Step to the rear, please, gentlemen. Step to the rear." One passenger said, "We're not gentlemen, we're comrades." "Impossible," said the conductor. "Comrades don't ride streetcars. They have big black automobiles."

After their meeting at Yalta, Roosevelt, Churchill and Stalin were driving along a country road when they ran into a cow that blocked the path of their automobile. Roosevelt, who had been a successful farmer, tried his best to get the cow to move, but was unsuccessful. Churchill issued some crisp commands in superb English, but the cow continued to refuse to budge. Stalin got out of the automobile and whispered to the cow. It promptly ran away. Roosevelt asked him: "How did you do it?" Stalin answered: "I told the cow I'd put her in the Communist Party."

A commissar was making a periodic check-up on the farms in his district. He stopped one peasant in the fields to inquire about the production on his turnip crop. "There has never been a crop to equal this, thanks to the glorious plan of our leaders," the peasant retorted. "If we were to place all our turnips in a pile, they would stretch to the very feet of God." The commissar was indignant. "But you know there is no God!" he roared. "Ah," smiled the peasant. "But there are no turnips either."

A simple peasant woman wearing a golden cross on a chain was asked by a Soviet policeman, "Why on earth do you wear that crazy fancy stuff around your neck?" "Why, to show those rotten Capitalists that we have complete religious freedom, of course."

Two small boys in Russia were caught in a thunderstorm and hid under a tree. They were very scared, and one of them suggested that they ought to say a prayer. "But we haven't been taught any prayers," objected the other. "Never mind," answered his friend. "We've been taught the alphabet and if we say it out loud, God will surely know how to make it into a prayer."

It happened at a Communist Party meeting at a small agricultural community in the Ukraine. The Chairman had finished his speech and the usual debates followed. One of the Party members raised his hand to obtain the right to speak quickly and shouted,"Long live Comrade Chervenov." He was warned by the chairman to wait because there were other comrades who had asked to speak earlier. But the impatient one seemed to have no time to wait. A few minutes later he again announced that he wanted to speak and repeated, "Long live Comrade Chervenov." Again he was called to order by the chairman who became irritated. At last he got permission to speak and everybody was awaiting tensely to hear what he had to say. But the comrade only exclaimed, "Long live Comrade Chervenov on my monthly salary of thirty rubles — I would like to see how long he could live on it."

A newspaper man was preparing to flee to the West from Russia. A friend asked him why. "There are two reasons," the newspaper man said. "First the regime might change and all my friends might be killed." "That is impossible," said the friend. "There you are," the newspaper man replied. "I told you I had two reasons."

When the general election took place, the workers and employees were led to the polls by Activists who handed them envelopes to be deposited in the ballot box. One worker who was more curious than the others opened his envelope to examine the ballot slip. "What are you doing there?" shouted an Activist. "I'd just like to find out for whom I'm voting," the worker replied. "You confounded fool — don't you know that that's a secret ballot?"

The village priest and the Communist Party secretary have known each other for years and occasionally would meet to chat. One day the secretary asked the priest: "How is it that every time you ring the bells so many people come running whether it's for Mass or Vespers or whatever, but when I send out a call for a meeting or a demonstration, no one shows up?" "I'll tell you the secret," replied the priest. "Like you, we promise the people a chance for Paradise. But the big difference is that we don't let them see it on earth."

Two Moscow citizens noticed a man carrying a flag down the street. One said to the other, "Is it a holiday?" "No, he carries the flag in order to know how the wind is blowing."

A worker was asked to volunteer to prove his devotion to the Soviet Union by leaping to his death in Red Square from the top of the Kremlin. He did, and was astounded to see that a net had been spread below the building, in order to save him. The officials who complimented him on his achievement asked him why he had volunteered to give his life on behalf of the Soviet Union. "To the devil with this life," he said.

In a Russian village an old man was praying in a church. A Communist official walked over and tapped him on the shoulder and said, "Old man, you ought to be ashamed of praying in our day and age." The old man turned and answered, "But I am praying for Khrushchev." "For Khrushchev? Well that's different," said the Communist. Then after some thinking, he asked: "And why is it you're praying for Khrushchev?" "You see, my son," said the old man, "under the royal family we had to pray for the Tsar and you know what happened. Now I am praying for Khrushchev, trusting in God's mercy."

Two Communist officials were talking about a problem they had in getting an oven built. "We have no problem about the delivery of the bricks for construction of the oven. The problem is where to get the clay for the manufacture of the bricks!"

Two Leningrad workers were talking. One said, "I'd like to ask you a riddle. Why is the atmosphere in our country like electric energy?" His friend said, "Tell me." The answer was, "Because the tension is high, the resistance is strong, and nobody can touch the conductor!"

The delegate of a district educational department visited a school. He asked a little boy, "Can you tell me how the world in which we live came into being?" After a few minutes of hesitation, the boy answered, "The world was created by God." "You are a stupid reactionary scamp. Sit down," shouted the delegate. "Now children, who is able to give me the correct answer?" Little Ivan put up his hand and the angry comrade called on him to answer the question. "It is true that the world was created by God, but prior to that, several famous Soviet scientists had concerned themselves with this problem!"

Speaking on economic affairs at a meeting of workers, a Communist Party propagandist said, "Our aim is to catch up with and overtake the United States." One worker whispered to a colleague, "When we catch up with the United States, they can let me off there and go on without me."

The surprise inspection is a very important part of the Soviet machinery. One inspector called a factory: "Hello, this is the inspector. The day after tomorrow, around two o'clock I'll be around for a surprise inspection."

An old woman dashed into a subway station and just managed to get into the train before it pulled out of the station. She sighed, "Thank God!" A soldier who was standing near her heard her and went over to the old lady and said, "No, citizen, you should say 'Thank Stalin for permitting me to get into the subway.'" The woman nodded thoughtfully and rode on. After a few minutes, she turned to the soldier and asked, "What will I say if Stalin dies?" The soldier thought for a moment and said, "Then you can say, 'Thank God.'"

A butcher in Moscow had three frankfurters on display. A customer came in and said he wanted to buy some frankfurters. The butcher said, "I'm sorry, but those frankfurters in the window are only there for display." The customer said, "That's all right, I'll take them even though they have been in the window." The butcher answered, "In that case, come back in ten days when we change the window display."

Two Russian citizens were asking about the latest Russian peace campaign. One asked, "Will there be war?" His friend answered: "No, but there will be such fighting about peace that no stone will remain unturned."

Radio Armenia reports that there are only three occasions when it is comfortable to sit on a hedgehog. One is when the animal has been shaved, another is when you are wearing tin pants, and the third is when the Party orders you to do it.

Pravda had the difficult job of reporting a competition between an American Ford and a Soviet Pobeda car in which the Ford won in every single category. The next day, *Pravda* carried the following item: "The results of the motor car competition were not surprising. Our Pobeda placed second. The American Ford automobile ended in the last place but one."

The agriculture ministers of a number of different provinces in the Soviet Union met to discuss the current situation. They were very depressed. One of the ministers was speaking: "Our harvest prospects are very poor, our tractors have broken down, and manpower is very scarce. Things look very bleak." One of his colleagues tried to encourage him: "Cheer up. These difficulties are only temporary. There is no doubt that Communism will triumph in the end and spread throughout the whole world." The minister flung up his hands in horror. Looking quickly around, he whispered, "Please, even in jest, don't say things like that. Where would we import our grain from?"

A periodical offered a definition of the Supreme Soviet of the U.S.S.R. (The National Assembly). The definition was: "It consists of people, half of whom are totally incapable while the other half are capable of everything."

Coming back from a trip to Moscow, Chervenko bought Tsola a Soviet fan as a souvenir. As soon as she tried to use it, the fan broke into pieces. "But that is no way to use a Soviet fan," remonstrated Chervenko. "You must move your head and hold the fan still."

50

A Russian worker was very distressed to find that he had overslept and was late for work. In order to save time, he did not dress completely but carried his pants out of his apartment with him and ran off to the factory. He came home in the evening completely dejected. His wife asked, "Well, how did it go?" He answered, "Terrible. I was later than I ever was. Everyone stopped me in the street to ask me where I got the pants and to ask me if I could help them get a pair too."

A Muscovite went into the famous subway in Moscow. He waited and waited but no train came. He went over to another Muscovite, who was also patiently waiting, and asked "Where are those wonderful automated trains that I heard so much about? They are supposed to be so clean and light and airy and prompt." "You can't believe that capitalist propaganda," was the reply.

A man in Tashkent was waiting patiently in line to buy soap. When he got to the store, he discovered that there was no more soap. He said, philosophically, "Well, it isn't too bad. After all, I have no water at home. Think of how bad I would feel if I had soap and had no water."

Word of the many jokes told by Rabinovitch had come to the ears of Premier Khrushchev, who summoned Rabinovitch to see him. Premier Khrushchev complained: "You know that living conditions are better here than they ever have been. Why do you then tell jokes about me?" "I thought," Rabinovitch answered, "you summoned me because you wanted to hear my jokes, not tell me yours."

A listener asked Radio Armenia what to do in the case of atomic attack. The answer was: "Put on a shroud and walk slowly to the nearest cemetery." "Why slowly?" "So as not to cause panic."

In the year 1990 a boy in Moscow asked his grandfather what a queue was. The old man explained that back in 1964, butter was in short supply and people had to form a queue to get their ration. "Very well," said the boy. "What is butter?"

A Soviet citizen inquired at a store about the price of a particular brand of razor blades. He was told that each box of blades cost two rubles. He was indignant. "In the State drugstore, their price is one ruble." "Then go and buy it there." "But there are none in the State drugstore." "If I did not have any in stock, I would also sell them for one ruble."

A Communist census taker asked an old Russian villager his age. He replied, "I'm twenty-seven." This was so clearly false that the census official suggested that the old man either could not count or may have miscalculated. The old man said, "Well, I'm really seventy-two, but these last forty-five years since the Revolution — do you call this living?"

An American trade union official was talking with a high Soviet official in Moscow. The Soviet official asked "How much does an average American worker earn a month?" "About $600 a month," replied the American. "And how much does he need to live?" "About $550." "What does he do with the rest?" "Oh," said the American, "ours is a free country. He can do as he pleases, it's no concern of mine. Now you tell me, what does a Russian worker earn?" "100 Rubles." "And what does he need for essentials?" "150 Rubles." "But how does he make up the difference?" "Ours is a free country, too," said the Russian. "It's no concern of mine."

What money is the jolliest to travel with? Why, it is Russian money, because everybody laughs upon seeing it.

Two Russian citizens were looking at a monument erected in honor of the Soviet Premier Khrushchev. One said to the other, "There are two things wrong with it." The second asked, "What are they?" His friend answered, "In the first place, there is no inscription 'Rest in Peace' on it." "But Khrushchev isn't dead yet." "That's the second thing that is wrong."

A Russian delegate visiting China was exchanging experiences with his Chinese comrades. "How do you handle intellectuals in the Russian Communist Party?" asked a Chinese. "Very carefully," said the Russian. "We handle them just like eggs." The Chinese giggled in appreciation. "Very good. Just like us. We too handle intellectuals just like eggs. We bury them sixty years until they are good and rotten."

One of the provinces in the Soviet Union announced that there would be prizes for farmers who exceeded their quota of grain for the year. The first prize was a week in residence at the Kremlin, observing the activities of Premier Khrushchev. The second prize was two weeks vacation in the Kremlin, observing the activities of Premier Khrushchev. The third prize was three weeks vacation in the Kremlin, observing the activities of Premier Khrushchev.

A Moscow office worker came home from work unexpectedly and found his wife in the arms of another man. He ignored the stranger, but shouted, "What kind of wife are you, idling around the house and amusing yourself when everybody in the district has heard that the grocer has lemons today?"

The Soviets are very strict in their application of lodging space regulations. Large rooms must house substantial numbers of people. A teacher distributed pictures of Lenin to school children and instructed the children to tell their parents to hang them in their rooms. After a while, agents were sent to check the parents to find out whether the pictures had been displayed as instructed. A report came in that little Marcovich's parents had failed to comply with the order. "Why have your people at home not hung our beloved leader's picture on the wall as all the others have?" asked the teacher. "Very simple, Comrade Teacher," young Marcovich replied. "The others have walls but we have none." "How come?" "We live in the middle of the room."

In the Russian military drill, it is said that there are five different positions: Attention, Super-attention, Extra-attention, Hyper-attention and Party-attention.

At the end of a political meeting in a Soviet factory, the Communist orator invited questions. One laborer asked him,"Could you please tell us whether we are now living under social-ism, or is that something even worse?"

On a visit to India by Bulganin and Khrushchev, the Soviet leaders were traveling by car toward a destination in the country. On the way, the car was held up by a cow which did not want to budge. (In India, cows are sacred, and no one can touch them.) The cow defied all attempts of the driver to get past her. Khrushchev decided to get out to persuade the cow. Bulganin said, "It's no use. There's nothing doing." Khrushchev answered, "Don't forget that I managed to convince three oxen at Geneva. Why do you think I won't be able to convince this cow?"

An important dignitary visited Moscow because he had read that living conditions there were so good that a person could get anything he wanted. When it came time for dinner at the finest hotel in Moscow the dignitary ordered: "Elephant stew, please." The waiter said it would be served shortly. A few minutes later, however, the chef called the head waiter to the kitchen. "What's the matter," asked the waiter, "don't tell me there is no elephant." The chef shook his head, "Oh, we've got the elephant from the zoo, but there are no onions!"

A large number of rabbits were seeking to leave the Soviet Union in order to go to Poland. They were stopped at the border by the secret police and border guards who said, "Why are you leaving the country?" The rabbits answered, "The police have just ordered the arrest of every camel in the Soviet Union." The guard answered, "But you are not camels." The rabbits answered, "Try to tell that to the secret police."

Many concert performers in the Soviet Union have observed that they would have no trouble in getting an audience if they could only get as many listeners as there are eavesdroppers.

Minister Kozlov had a bad night. "I had a horrible dream," he confessed to a friend. "I dreamed that Comrade Premier Khrushchev asked for asylum in America." "That's not so bad. It was just a dream," his friend consoled him. "You are right," Kozlov said. "But when I dream things like that, what must Khrushchev be dreaming?"

Moscow circles were buzzing with a recipe for spiritual food. "Mix a heaping teaspoonful of Soviet internationalism with twelve ladles of heated Soviet patriotism. Season with anti-cosmopolitan spices and herbs. Then pour over a mixture of sweet syrup of infinite love for Khrushchev. Bake in a hot oven and serve quickly because these Soviet literary dishes go bad on cooling."

Two old friends were walking across Red Square in Moscow. There was nobody else in sight and the area was completely silent. One said to the other, "Shh." His friend asked, "Why, what's the matter?" He continued, "I didn't say anything, and there's no one here." His friend answered, "Don't you know, that wherever two Russians get together, one of them is bound to be from the police?"

Stalin fell into a pond and was going under water for the third time. A local farmer saw him, jumped in and pulled him out of the water and to safety. The dictator introduced himself and said, "You can have anything within my power to give you. Any reward is yours." The farmer said, "There is one thing you can do for me — don't tell anybody I saved you."

Sasha was talking to Tomas about the several five-year plans. "After the fifth year, everybody will have a bicycle. After the sixth year, every-one will have a car. By the seventh year, every Russian will have a jet plane." His friend asked, "What would I do with a jet plane?" "You fool," was the retort. "Suppose you hear they're going to have matches on sale in Vladivostok and you live in Kursk. So, you hop in your jet plane, and whoosh — you're first in line for the matches."

A peasant was marveling at his trip to Moscow. "They have big buildings that used to take two years to build that now go up in two months." "Yes," his friend answered. "And the ceme-teries that used to take fifty years to fill now are filled in a year."

There has been much discussion in the Soviet Union about the quality of the bread that is available. One morning Ivan met a man in the street who seemed to be covered with soot from head to toe. Believing the man to be a chimney sweep and because it is an old superstition that seeing a chimney sweep means good fortune, Ivan greeted him and said, "I will have good luck today." The man replied, "I beg your par-don, Comrade Ivan, but I am not a chimney sweep, I am a miller in the flour mill."

61

On a cold winter day a man walked along a snow-covered street in Kiev and muttered, "It's intolerable." Two secret policemen approached him and said, "You're under arrest." "Why?" the man stammered, "I have done nothing." "You have complained about the regime." "The regime? I only said the cold was intolerable." "You are lying," the policeman told him, "the cold is still tolerable."

Rabinovitch and Abramovitch are strolling through the streets of Warsaw in the year 1999. "Remember the good old days when we were young and spoke Russian?" Rabinovitch says sadly in Chinese.

Definition of an opportunist: someone who is learning to eat caviar with chopsticks.

A Russian traveler called Popov visited Poland and sent a postcard: "Greetings from free Warsaw." He next sent a message from Czechoslovakia: "Greetings from free Prague." From Bulgaria, he wrote: "Greetings from free Sofia." Then he wrote a postcard from Hungary: "Greetings from free Budapest." His final postcard from Vienna simply read: "Greetings from free Popov."